FUTURE TRANSPORT
ON LAND

By Steve Parker
Illustrations by David West

 **Marshall Cavendish**
Benchmark
New York

This publication represents the opinions and views of the author based on Steve Parker's personal experience, knowledge, and research. The information in this book serves as a general guide only. The author and publisher have used their best efforts in preparing this book, and disclaim liability rising directly and indirectly from the use and application of this book.

Other Marshall Cavendish Offices:
Marshall Cavendish International (Asia) Private Limited, 1 New Industrial Road, Singapore 536196 • Marshall Cavendish International (Thailand) Co Ltd. 253 Asoke, 12th Flr, Sukhumvit 21 Road, Klongtoey Nua, Wattana, Bangkok 10110, Thailand • Marshall Cavendish (Malaysia) Sdn Bhd, Times Subang, Lot 46, Subang Hi-Tech Industrial Park, Batu Tiga, 40000 Shah Alam, Selangor Darul Ehsan, Malaysia

Marshall Cavendish is a trademark of Times Publishing Limited

Copyright © 2011 David West Children's Books

Library of Congress Cataloging-in-Publication Data

Parker, Steve, 1952-
On land / Steve Parker.
p. cm. -- (Future transport)
Includes bibliographical references and index.
Summary: "Gives a concise history of travel by land, water, air, or in space, showing the technology available today, in the near future, and in centuries to come"--Provided by publisher.
ISBN 978-1-60870-779-9 (print)
1. Motor vehicles--Juvenile literature. 2. Automobile travel--Juvenile literature. I. Title.
TL147.P368 2012
388.3'4--dc22

2011000999

Produced by
David West 🏃 Children's Books
7 Princeton Court
55 Felsham Road
London SW15 1AZ

Designer: Gary Jeffrey
Illustrator: David West

The photographs in this book are used by permission and through the courtesy of:
Abbreviations: t-top, m-middle, b-bottom, r-right, l-left, c-center.
title page, 30b, Franco Vairani/MIT Smart Cities; 6t, Roby, 6r, David Ingham, 6bl, Stephen Foskett; 7t, RUD66, 7tr, Karrmann, 7ml, Mark Brown, 7mr, Sirsnapsalot; 8t, Anatoly Shikhov, 8mr, TheAlieness GiselaGiardinoÇ?, 8b, 20t, Peugeot; 9t, 19m, General Motors, 9bl, Peugeot RD concept / Carlos Arturo Torres // PSA peugeot, 9br, Mytho88; 10t, Kevin Ward, 10m, Christopher Pollard, 10br, Thomas doerfer, 10bl, Tamas Siklosi; 11t, Franco Corral / Honda R&D, 11m, Hennessey Performance, 11b, Dmitry Valberg; 12t, Thomas Schoch, 12ml, Adam Palethorpe, 12mr, Modec UK, 12bl, Hugo Plazas; 13tl, Ford Motor Co, 13ml, HaiShang Design, 13mr, 13b, Volvo AB; 14tl, Shenzhen Hashi Future Parking Equipment Co., Ltd, 14m, ULTra PRT, 14l, Gabriel Wartofsky, 14b, acnatta; 16l, Rs1421; 17m, Priestmangoode, 17b, Bombardier Transportation; 18t, © Bombardier Recreational Products inc. (BRP). All rights reserved., 18m, Nufkin, 18bl, Alvinodesign, 18br, Shweeb Holdings Ltd; 19tl, Jonathunder, 19tr, Charles01, 19br, HotDuckZ; 20m, Eric F Savage; 21t, Carbon Motors Corp., 21bl, Adam Schacter Design Ltd, 21br, Robert Engelmann; 22t, Daimler AG, 22m, Volvo Cars, 22ml, Thesupermat, 22b, Bosch, 22bl, Saab; 23tr, Rennett Stowe; 23m, Michelin Challenge Design/Goran Marinkovic; 24t, BMW of North America, LLC, 24m, PSA Peugeot Citroën, 24b, Siemens AG, Munich/Berlin; 25t, Matthias Hensel; 26t, Argonne National Laboratory, 26m, U. S. Air Force photo by Sue Sapp, 26bl, Brian Snelson; 27tr, Peter Van den Bossche, 27l, Hideki Kimura, Kohei Sagawa, 27m, Mariordo Mario Roberto Duran Ortiz, 27mr, El monty; 28t, Nicolas Stone, 28ml, MITCHELL JOACHIM, 28l, Michael Chia-Liang Lin/MIT Smart Cities group; 30t, Mazda R&D of North America/Matthew Cunningham

Printed in China
135642

Contents

INTRODUCTION

"Good evening, driver. Please enter your identity code and destination. Sit comfortably in your virtual safety bubble and activate the anti-collision force field. Now power up the fuel cells for low-hover mode. CityCentral computer says Freeway 17 is busy and advises we take Highpass F9. If you are ready, let's ride!"

Land transport has such a massive effect on what we do every day, from city cars to racy sportscars, tough SUVs, cruising limousines, school buses, roaring trucks, and crowded subways. Road and rail seem to rule our lives.

People want sleeker, speedier, smoother, more convenient. But how long can it last? Fuels based on petroleum are running out. Highway safety is a massive issue. Vehicles clog the routes and exhaust fumes dim the skies. Travel across the land must become smarter, cleaner, and greener.

Getting motivated

In the beginning, travel relied on leg muscles—human, as well as donkeys, horses, camels, even elephants. Then came the motorcar and the world really got moving.

In 1770 Nicolas Cugnot made a steam wagon (left) but it crashed. The first true automobile was Karl Benz's Motorwagon of 1885 (top).

Horseless Carriages

The steam engine was the first mobile power plant. From the 1820s it propelled railroad locomotives. Mass land transport began, but only where the rails went. Several inventors tried to adapt horse-drawn carriages to steam. However, the internal combustion or gasoline engine powered the first successful road vehicles.

Steam ruled the rails for more than a century. The fastest steam locomotive was the UK's Mallard at 126 mph (203 km/h) in 1938.

As well as four wheels, keen riders tried to modify bicycles of the day, like the the "penny-farthing," into early motorcycles.

In the 1910s steam made a partial comeback with speedy autos like the Stanley Steamer. But gasoline engines then took over.

6

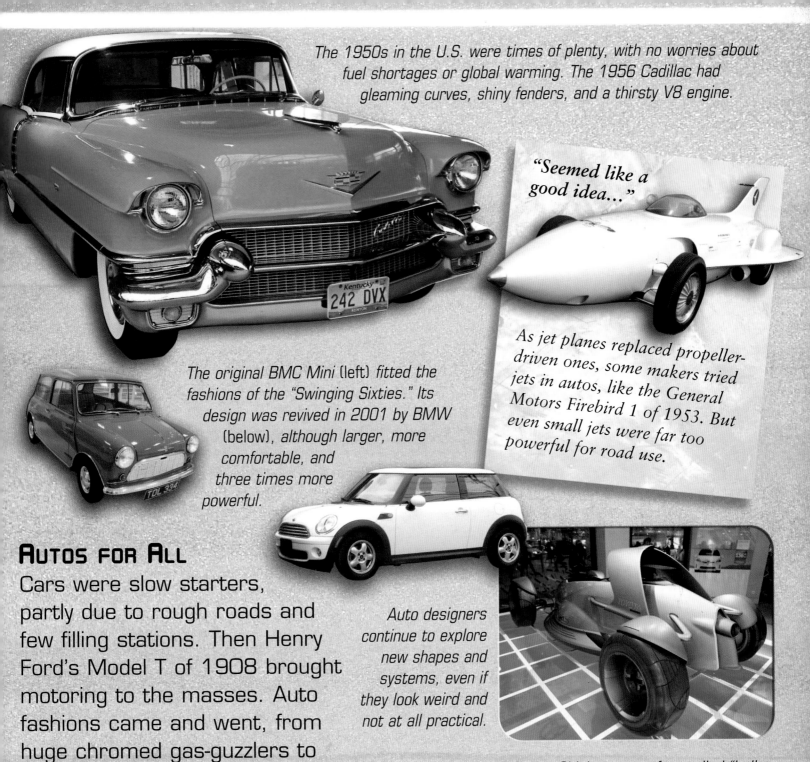

The 1950s in the U.S. were times of plenty, with no worries about fuel shortages or global warming. The 1956 Cadillac had gleaming curves, shiny fenders, and a thirsty V8 engine.

"Seemed like a good idea..."

The original BMC Mini (left) fitted the fashions of the "Swinging Sixties." Its design was revived in 2001 by BMW (below), although larger, more comfortable, and three times more powerful.

As jet planes replaced propeller-driven ones, some makers tried jets in autos, like the General Motors Firebird 1 of 1953. But even small jets were far too powerful for road use.

Autos for All

Cars were slow starters, partly due to rough roads and few filling stations. Then Henry Ford's Model T of 1908 brought motoring to the masses. Auto fashions came and went, from huge chromed gas-guzzlers to the sports supercars and compact city cars of today.

Auto designers continue to explore new shapes and systems, even if they look weird and not at all practical.

In 1964 Japan's O Series Shinkansens, often called "bullet trains," brought a new era to rail travel. Drawing electricity from overhead power lines, they had a top speed of more than 140 mph (225 km/h). Other countries quickly took up the idea of high-speed rail services.

CITY SLICKERS

Some city vehicles spend more time standing still in traffic, belching fumes, than on the move. The future city auto will probably be small, smart, and electric.

PARK, PLUG, AND PLAY

Electric autos still use energy to recharge their batteries, of course. But it is made at the electricity generating station, which is many times more efficient than every vehicle having its own gasoline engine. It is also quieter and less polluting, and saves valuable petroleum for more important uses.

French automaker Peugot's Capca urban two-seater has electric in-wheel motors, transparent solar panels for windows, and fits a recharging hub.

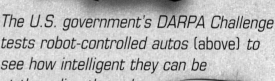

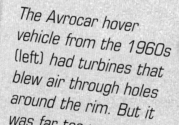

The Avrocar hover vehicle from the 1960s (left) had turbines that blew air through holes around the rim. But it was far too unstable.

The U.S. government's DARPA Challenge tests robot-controlled autos (above) to see how intelligent they can be at threading through city streets and slow traffic.

Peugot's hi-tech electric BB1 MicroCar (left), with four seats and baggage room, recalls the "bubble cars" of the 1950s such as the Italian Isetta (above).

Dual sun roof

Panoramic windshield

Hydrogen gas tanks

45kW fuel cell stack

16 kW Li-ion battery pack

268-hp electric drive motor

CHRYSLER ECOVOYAGER

The ecoVoyager will carry four people and baggage. Its electric motor can be powered by Li-ion rechargeable cells or an electricity-generating hydrogen fuel cell, for a range of 300 miles (483 km).

"Seemed like a good idea..."

The flying auto looked set for take-off in 1947 when the ConVairCar 118 was demonstrated to the public. But a crash wrecked the car section. Bad publicity meant the program was canceled.

PUSHING THE LIMITS

A key area for future research is better battery performance. Today's Li-ion (lithium ion) rechargeable batteries, or secondary cells, take several hours to re-energize and limit range to 200 to 300 miles (322–483 km). A solution could be a replaceable charged battery pack to swap with the discharged one.

Nissan's Pivo2 is an electric car with a passenger pod that swivels around, eliminating the need for reversing.

The RD city car's three wheels make it extra-maneuverable for parking as well as being fun to drive (left).

IN THE FAST LANE

The Dodge ZEO "muscle car" stands for Zero Emissions Operation. It is all-electric but its powerful shape recalls the V8-powered roadsters of the 1960s.

Almost as soon as automobiles were invented, people with lots of money wanted the latest, fastest, coolest, most glamorous designs. In years to come, with the focus on economy, low-energy, and eco-friendly, can these show-off supercars survive?

New Standards

Like many autos, the next generation of sportscars may be hybrid or all-electric. Then the task will be getting the most out of batteries and electric motors. In 2008 the Tesla Roadster set the early standard for electric production models, managing 0 to 60 mph (0–97 km) in 3.7 seconds.

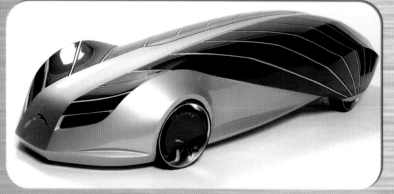

Luxury automaker Jaguar's XXI model, when parked, folds out its black solar panels. These face the Sun like leaves and recharge the onboard batteries.

"Seemed like a good idea..."

Bricklin's 1970s SV-1 sportscar was made from acrylic and fiberglass for safety and lightness. But it was slow, the body cracked easily, the engine overheated, and the maker went broke.

The Maybach Amphibious Luxury Vehicle could change both land and water travel. A luxury limo on land, its body extends sideways into a trimaran (three-hulled) watercraft with hard-panel solar sails.

SPEED DEMONS

Less weight and better streamlining, or aerodynamics, are also vital for top performance. Computers borrow shapes from aircraft and speedboats to help land vehicles slip swiftly through air yet keep their wheels firmly gripping the tarmac.

HONDA GREAT RACER

Engineering giant Honda proposes its Great Racer for an imaginary 2025 round-the-world contest by land, sea, and air. The vehicle senses terrain and changes mode automatically.

Cockpit

Roadwheels fold away in other modes

Rear roadwheels

Wing for airplane mode becomes hull in water

Nozzles for air or waterjet propulsion

Carbon-fiber composite materials keep the Hennessey Venom GT's weight to just over 1 ton (0.9 t). This 750-horsepower monster sells for about $600,000. One of the last supercars?

BMW's Vision EfficientDynamics has hybrid electric and turbo-diesel propulsion, and should do 0 to 60 mph (0–97 km) in 4.8 seconds.

TRUCKS AND UTILITIES

The hard-working freight and utility side of land transport will have a makeover in the next twenty-five years. More varied energy sources and intelligent electronics should keep daily life moving.

Australian "road-trains" will continue to roar through the outback, to supply remote communities with vital supplies such as fuels.

ROAD WARRIORS

Trucks move essential freight across the nation, while utilities fulfil day-to-day tasks like store deliveries and garbage collection. These big workhorses can benefit from new technologies such as dedicated road space and faster turnarounds.

Scania's city utility vehicle will have a diesel-electric hybrid engine, a "friendly" appearance, and wheel cover displays that show it is being driven safely.

Modec electric trucks dash quietly around urban streets, with a range of 150 miles (240 km). The powerful electric motor has just three moving parts for easy servicing.

German designer Luigi Colani's "organic" shapes for new trucks use curves to lower drag or wind resistance.

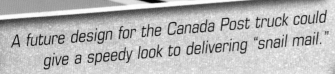

A future design for the Canada Post truck could give a speedy look to delivering "snail mail."

Ford's Nucleon concept from 1958 had a small nuclear reactor. It was designed to cover an amazing 5,000 miles (8,000 km) on one fuel charge, but was too expensive to produce.

INFRASTRUCTURE

Land transport relies on infrastructure such as smooth roads, filling stations, rest stops, and traffic control. A big stuck truck can waste more energy than thirty family autos. Dedicated freight lanes could reduce pollution and gasoline use, as faster vehicles pass by.

Stilt-legged supertrucks carry their load in a massive scoop for extra-rapid tipping. The driver has a bird's-eye view.

All-around bubble cab

Volvo suggest a 2020 Green Roads system where often-stopping service vehicles and mass transits are separate from private autos.

FUTURE ARTICULATED DUMPER

Volvo's idea for the next-generation dump truck includes a cab that tilts forward so the driver can climb in easily, and a tip body that telescopes rearward to keep the load low.

Front body section slides into rear

Articulated cab-body joint

13

PEOPLE MOVERS

To save energy and reduce pollution, nations look to more public transport and better mass transit. However, to tempt people to use them, they should be clean, frequent, fast, inexpensive, safe, reliable, comfortable—and on time.

The Straddling Bus proposal is two highways for the price of one. Smaller private and utility autos stay below while passengers ride high in cabins with stiltlike sides.

London's Heathrow Airport uses small, battery-powered, four-person pods called Personal Rapid Transits, PRTs. They run in trough-shaped guideways.

ROAD AND RAIL

Mass transits include buses and coaches on the road, also various rails such as subways, elevated railroads, and monorails. Electricity will continue to be the main power source since it is convenient, quiet, and low-polluting. But it could be generated by mixed wind, solar, hydro, and fuels.

The Icon Bus could run in Santa Monica, California. Inspired by the red double-deckers of London, England, its huge windows offer great views.

NABI (North American Bus Industries) supplies the latest low-energy vehicles, including those fueled by compressed natural gas.

"Seemed like a good idea…"

Vacuum-tube propulsion uses low air pressure or a partial vacuum in front, and high air pressure behind, to push vehicles through a huge tube. But passengers would suffer burst eardrums and serious breathing problems!

CENTRAL CONTROL

Vital to city transit systems is a central computer for the road sign displays, traffic lights, and remote-controlled vehicles such as buses and monorails. Future computers should be able to switch traffic from one route to another soon after an accident or blockage, to avoid gridlock and keep the city moving.

Lots of stops very close together shifts the focus from travel time to time spent loading and unloading. Fast, easy access needs extra-wide doors, with the transit floor at the same level as the boarding platform.

INSIDE TRACK

The first mechanized land transports were railroads, almost 200 years ago. Long gone are puffing steam engines. What does the future hold for the "iron road"?

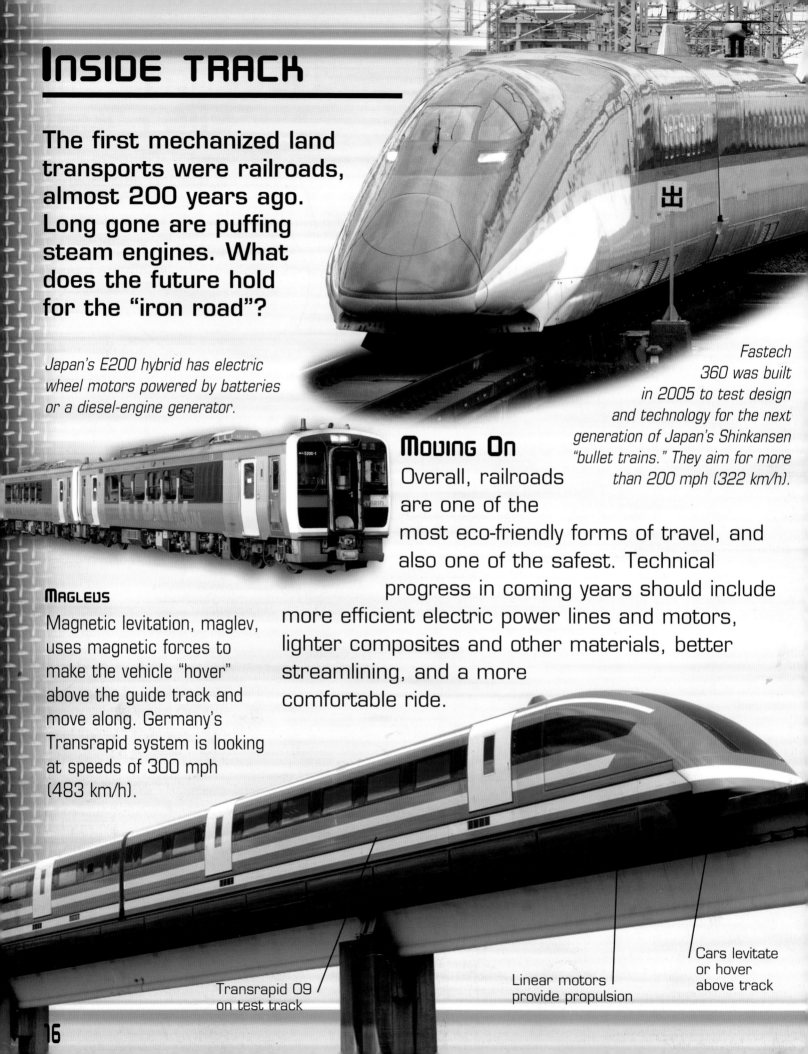

Japan's E200 hybrid has electric wheel motors powered by batteries or a diesel-engine generator.

Fastech 360 was built in 2005 to test design and technology for the next generation of Japan's Shinkansen "bullet trains." They aim for more than 200 mph (322 km/h).

Moving On

Overall, railroads are one of the most eco-friendly forms of travel, and also one of the safest. Technical progress in coming years should include more efficient electric power lines and motors, lighter composites and other materials, better streamlining, and a more comfortable ride.

Maglevs

Magnetic levitation, maglev, uses magnetic forces to make the vehicle "hover" above the guide track and move along. Germany's Transrapid system is looking at speeds of 300 mph (483 km/h).

Cars levitate or hover above track

Linear motors provide propulsion

Transrapid 09 on test track

PERSONALIZED RAIL

Railroad cars rarely stop by your door or even at the end of your street. PRRT, Personal Road-Rail Transport, could be a solution. People would drive their small electric autos to the nearest rail stop and onto low-load wagons. Here they plug in to recharge the auto's batteries, relax, then drive off to their destination.

"Seemed like a good idea…"

THE GEORGE BENNIE RAILPLANE SYSTEM OF TRANSPORT

Swift Safe Sure

Scottish inventor George Bennie's Railplane from the 1930s used an aircraft-like propeller, and guide rails above and below. It was to "fly" above slower freight railcars. It never took off.

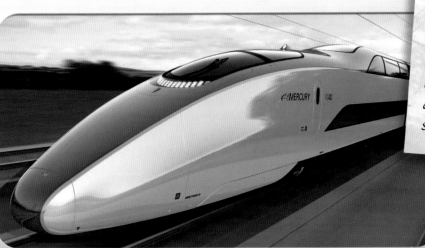

The Mercury double-deck high-speed train could run at 225 mph (362 km/h) on UK rails within twenty years. It uses electric, low-carbon technology with a sleek shape, private compartments reserved for group travel, and even a mini shopping mall.

Las Vegas, Nevada, has a monorail track almost 4 miles (6 km) long, with seven stations. There are plans to build an extension out to McCarran International Airport.

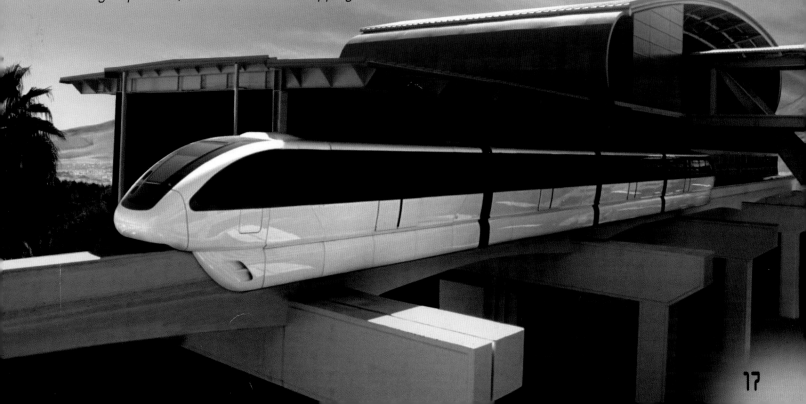

Personal Transport

Most land trips are just one person, or maybe two. So taking a big multiseat vehicle is an obvious waste of fuel and other resources. How small and neat can personal transport, PT, become?

Could the future be one-wheeled? The Embrio BRP monocycle idea is hydrogen fuel-cell powered and auto-balanced by gyroscopes.

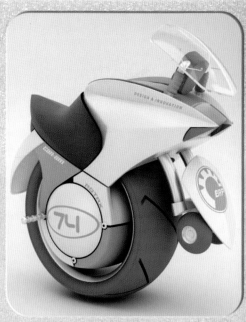

Maybe three wheels is the way forward with Honda's 3R-C one-person electric tricycle. The bubble roof folds away in nice weather.

Nimble Nippers

Bicycles are "green" PTs and great for health. But they can be cold, windy, rainy, and tiring. And no matter how careful the rider is, they are at risk from other road users. Future PTs should keep out the weather, use energy carefully, and give good protection, too.

Alvino Design's Proxima blurs the border between auto and motorcycle. Its wrap-around cabin sits above hot-rod style wheels for a fast, fun trip.

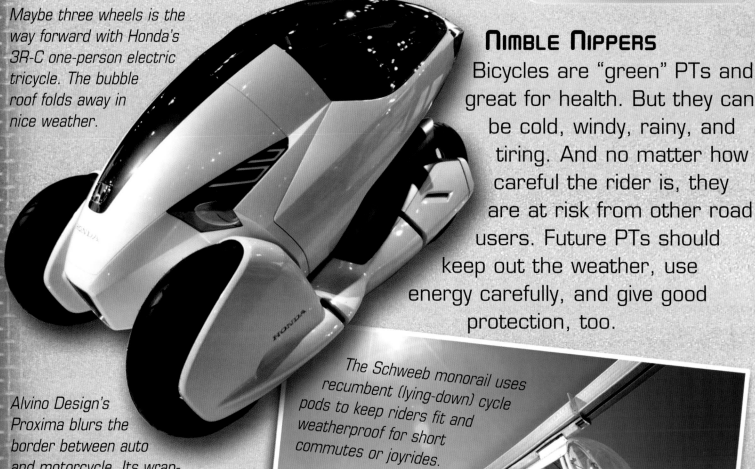

The Schweeb monorail uses recumbent (lying-down) cycle pods to keep riders fit and weatherproof for short commutes or joyrides.

Comms

Cities will continue to grow in coming years, so urban PTs are predicted as a growth area. Wireless (radio) networks will give drivers the latest on weather, accidents and other problems, and even advise the best battery-recharging plan.

GM-SA EN-V

General Motors–Shanghai Automotive suggest developing the Segway as a two-wheeled, two-person urban EN–V, Electric-Networked Vehicle. It will communicate in real time with GPS satellites and local wireless networks.

Mini-monocycles may become a fun fashion item. After the trip, they could be sent away to park automatically.

Nearby–object sensors

One motor per wheel

Gryo-balanced cabin

Emergency Vehicles

Speed kills—but it can also save. The faster the emergency services reach the scene, the more people they will be able to rescue and treat.

Peugeot's H2O firefighting truck will use a fuel cell to make electricity to power the drive motors and the pump for water in the huge rear tank.

Race Against Time

In any emergency, whether a wildfire, a cardiac arrest, or a road accident, the first minutes are critical. But the route to get there can be rough and remote, or jammed with traffic. Future emergency vehicles need extra power, heavy-duty mechanics and suspension, and tough tires.

This future fire truck has all-terrain grip and heat-resistant bodywork. It will carry 570 gallons (2,158 l) of water plus chemicals for foam impulse-cannons.

"Seemed like a good idea…"

In 2003 this 1940s Ford ambulance was fitted with a GE J79 jet engine—the same one that powers the MD F-4 Phantom airplane. The ambulance reaches 200 mph (322 km/h) but sadly it is not licensed for ordinary roads.

Carbon Motors E7 Squad Car

Instead of modifying a standard auto, the E7 is the first police vehicle designed exactly for that purpose. It has bullet-proof doors, a clean-burn dual-turbo diesel engine, and all-around video and audio recording.

Flush police lights

Rear-hinged rear door

Strong bull-bar fenders

Each rear seat belt is anchored in the center with the buckle near the door, so the officer does not need to reach across a prisoner.

The E7's front seats are extra-wide to fit the officer's gun belt, and comfortable for long duty times.

Help from HQ

Emergencies need fast communications. Live video and sound will be relayed from the scene back to headquarters. There, experts can give best advice to on-the-spot workers, such as how to save an injury victim or even defuse a bomb.

The Ford Rescue-X go-anywhere vehicle carries a medical module with scanner and computer-aided surgical set-up.

Rough ground, swamps, and water would be no problem for the ARC, Amphibious Rescue Craft. It is planned for flooded and hurricane-hit regions.

21

SAFETY FIRST

Speed is fun, looks are cool, eco-friendly is good—but safety is first. Can land transport accidents and injuries keep going down?

SOFTEN THE BLOW

One of the main in-vehicle safety developments has been the airbag. It was first seen for drivers in Mercedes Benz sedans in 1981. Next came passenger bags, then rear-seat ones. Latest is the side–curtain air bag. Self-inflating shoulder-harness restraints may follow.

The driver airbag inflates in a split second (above) when vehicle sensors detect sudden deceleration or slowing down. It prevents the driver smashing into the steering wheel or windshield. Mercedes Benz side–curtain airbags (left) will cushion impacts from the left or right.

The latest Volvos feature sensors that warn of nearby oncoming objects.

The Saab active head restraint cups around the head to stop it rebounding forward and causing whiplash injuries.

Bosch Night Vision's near-infrared light shines at the scene in front. A camera near the rear-view mirror picks up the reduced-glare reflections and displays them on the screen.

Prevention Systems

Around-vehicle advances will include infrared, radar, and microwave sensors to detect oncoming objects and flash up warning displays or sounds. This should get rid of the "blind spots" that trouble drivers, especially when overtaking at speed on the freeway at night.

"Seemed like a good idea..."

The 1948 Tucker "Torpedo" had many ahead-of-its-time safety features including a swiveling central headlamp, seat belts, padded dash, and all-around safety cage. But the company had bribery, security, and tax scandals. Only 51 Torpedoes were made.

Scarab-E's "cocoon" body of advanced composite materials will be light yet strong, for all-around protection. Inner sensors "feel" the driver's mood and monitor any suspicious driver reactions.

Virtual Safety Bubble

The virtual safety bubble is an all-around array of sensors using different technologies. They register any nearby object, predict its direction and speed, and let the driver know. If the driver fails to act, automatically the vehicle takes the best avoiding action.

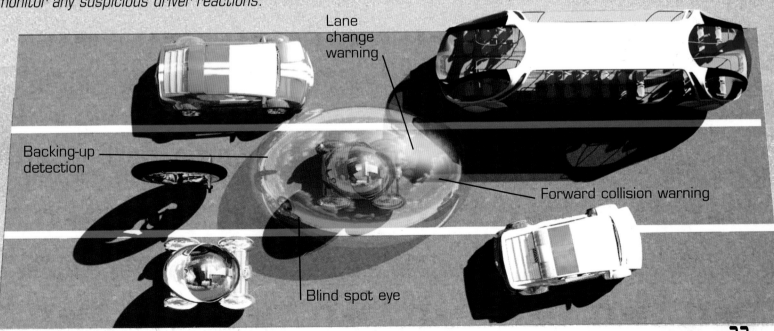

Lane change warning

Backing-up detection

Forward collision warning

Blind spot eye

FABULOUS FABRICATIONS

BMW's GINA has a fabric body skin pulled over a skeleton of adjustable metal and carbon-fiber wires.

Being eco-friendly out on the road is great. But a huge amount of eco-harm can be done before this, during manufacture. Automakers should reduce their use of energy and raw materials.

Laser-beam welding of steel and aluminum is becoming more accurate and faster. The beam tip can be less than 1/50th of an inch (0.5 mm).

ROBOTS AND MATERIALS

Future factories will have even more robots, automatic equipment, and computers than today. Every bit of waste, such as leftovers from drilling and trimming, will be recycled back into the production process. Non-rust materials such as composites, resins, and plastics are set to become lighter yet stronger.

Robots do not take time out for vacations, sickness, or even coffee. But they must be kept well maintained, adjusted, and controlled. The role of their human "carers" will be increasingly important.

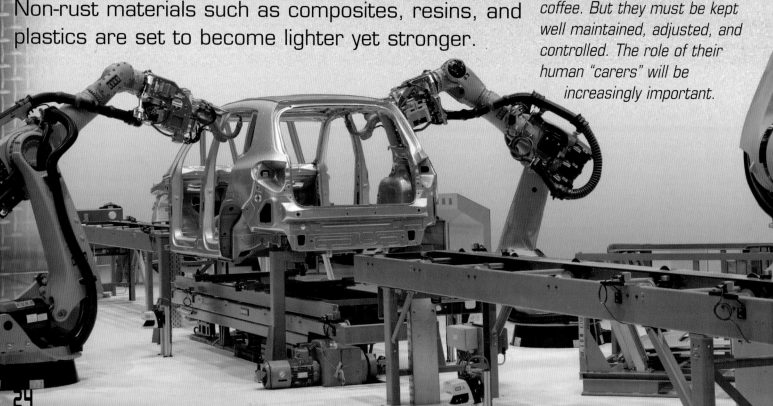

SMART PRODUCTION

There could also be progress on the assembly line. Vehicles will be designed from sets of standard units and modules, fitted together in different combinations. The assembly line will quick-switch to make individual vehicles, colors, and personalized features, according to each customer's order.

VW's "Auto City" factory and theme park at Wolfsburg, Germany, has giant storage silos for 400 new cars. Buyers can watch their vehicles being collected by revolving elevator.

Where are the people? In the distant future they may only appear on the assembly line for regular maintenance.

POWER TO THE WHEELS

The Tesla Roadster was the first road-legal all-electric car to go into volume production. It covers 220 miles (354 km) on a charge of its Li-ion batteries.

Land transport will probably use an increasing range of fuels, motors, and engines, depending on the vehicle type and its main role for work or leisure.

Ways to Go

After many years of false starts, electric autos are at last making headway. Some are all-electric using current from rechargeable batteries or hydrogen fuel cells. Others are series hybrid with an added combustion engine that also generates electricity. In partial hybrids either the engine or the motor turns the wheels.

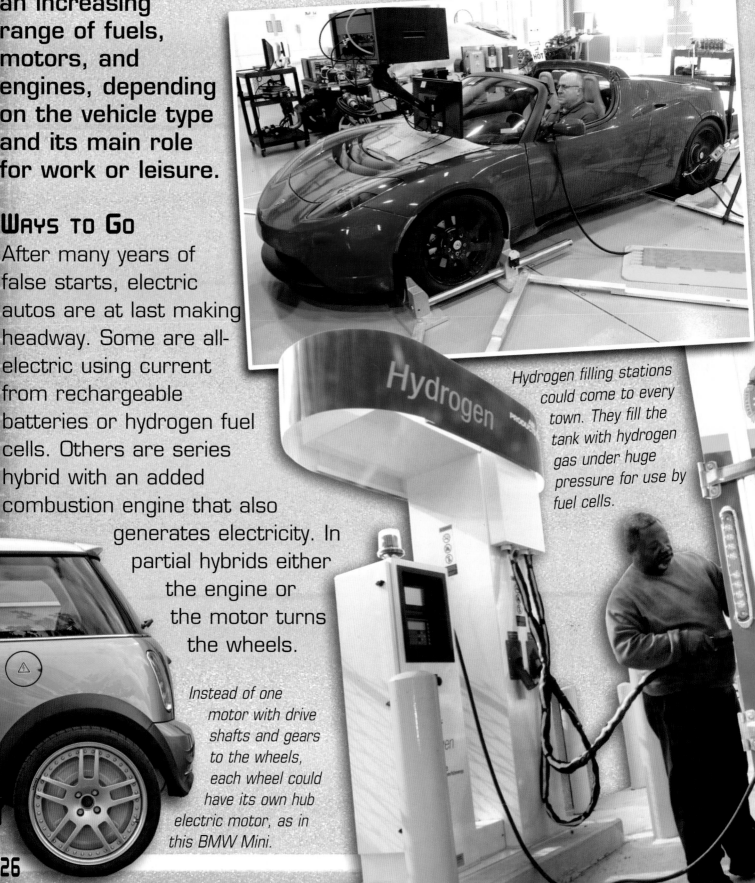

Hydrogen filling stations could come to every town. They fill the tank with hydrogen gas under huge pressure for use by fuel cells.

Instead of one motor with drive shafts and gears to the wheels, each wheel could have its own hub electric motor, as in this BMW Mini.

FUTURE FUELS

Biofuels are made from sustainable crops such as sugarcane or canola. But with so many hungry people, there are arguments about whether farmland should grow human food instead. Solar panels are improving fast and, one day, vehicle bodies and windows made from them may help to charge batteries.

"Seemed like a good idea..."

In 1996 GM's EV1 was an all-electric auto designed to test engineering, marketing, and driving of electric vehicles. It worked well, then U.S. laws on carbon emissions changed. All 800 EV1s were either crushed or sent to museums and auto collections.

Tokai University, Japan, won the South African Solar Challenge in 2008 and 2010. These contests develop solar panel technology.

Electric generator

Electric motor

Gasoline tank

Li-ion battery packs in floor

Gasoline engine

MDI's AirPod runs on air! That is, very high-pressure air let out slowly to turn its road wheels.

INSIDE THE CHEVROLET VOLT

The Chevy Volt hybrid has mains-rechargeable Li-ion batteries for its electric drive motor. As these run down, the small four-cylinder gasoline engine kicks in to turn a generator for current to the drive motor and for battery recharging.

The Chevrolet Volt went on sale in 2010.

JAM-FREE FUTURE

Hyundai's 2020 family auto is covered with solar panels that make electricity to turn water into hydrogen for its fuel cells.

Parking mode

Travel mode

Predictions say that around the world each day, there will be 70,000 more vehicles—mainly in Asia. How can roads, parking, and other infrastructure cope with such massive growth?

Vehicles like this MIT Soft Car will learn about their cities and help their people to travel more efficiently.

MORE VARIETY

One solution is more kinds of vehicles. Small electric pod-type autos for two or three people would be common in cities. Medium-sized hybrid autos will carry families. Increasing fuel prices, more traffic controls, and stricter pollution laws could shift long-distance land travel from road to rail.

ROBOSCOOTER

The electric RoboScooter could be ideal for city errands or short commutes to and from the workplace. Quiet and clean, it folds up to reduce its ground area or "footprint" and save space, for parking and recharging.

MIT's electric City Cars could stack against each other when not in use, much like shopping carts. This idea would reduce congestion, pollution, and urban energy waste.

In thirty years cities could have all kinds of different transports, mostly powered by electricity. This would be generated from sustainable alternative technologies such as solar and wind.

NETWORK CITY

Communications will also play their part. Vehicles linked to the Internet can route around traffic jams and gather information about their passsengers' regular journeys. Autos on highways may lock into a "virtual" driving train or convoy, to keep their distance automatically as some leave and others join.

LOOK FURTHER!

In the distant future, perhaps 100 years from now, will we still have land transport? Inventions such as antigravity drives could mean that everyone goes by air. But some people may still want the thrill of speeding down the freeway.

The Mazda Motonari idea is a fully adjustable vehicle suit worn by the driver. Covered with solar cells, it moves on four roller-wheels, and changes shape for different conditions and journeys.

Road transport could gradually change into air transport, with hovercars and hoverbikes. Highways become leftovers from the past.

Glossary

Biofuels
Fuels (energy sources) made from biological or living substances such as oil from crops, or gas from rotting matter—and even dried animal dung!

Composites
Materials made from several substances like plastics, carbon or glass fibers, resins, and ceramics.

Fuel Cell
A device that makes electricity from fuel such as hydrogen by splitting its atoms apart. It produces water as the main by-product.

Infrastructure
Supporting systems and networks, which for land vehicles include roads, bridges, tunnels, gas stations, parking lots, and traffic control.

Gyroscope
A fast-spinning device that keeps its position and resists being moved.

Hybrid
A vehicle or craft with two forms of propulsion, such as a gasoline engine and an electric motor.

Maglev
Magnetic levitation, using magnetic forces of attraction (pulling together) or repulsion (pushing apart) to make a vehicle "float" or levitate.

Monorail
A vehicle that rides on one central rail, rather than two rails side by side as in the standard railroad.

Secondary Cells
Electricity-making cells or "batteries" that are rechargeable, rather than primary cells which are not.

Shinkansen
Japanese railroad electric cars, often called "bullet trains" from their streamlined shape and fast speed.

Solar Cells and Panels
Button-sized electronic devices that turn light into electrical energy. Many solar cells in one large sheet are a solar panel (solar array).

Turbine
A rotating shaft with angled fan-shaped blades or rotors, which spin around when gases or liquids flow past them.

Index